YOUR KNOWLEDGE HAS VALUE

Marcus Kreysch

Behavioral Economics. Lernzusammenfassung

GRIN Verlag

Bibliografische Information der Deutschen Nationalbibliothek:

Die Deutsche Bibliothek verzeichnet diese Publikation in der Deutschen National-
bibliografie; detaillierte bibliografische Daten sind im Internet über http://dnb.d-
nb.de/ abrufbar.

Imprint:

Copyright © 2014 GRIN Verlag GmbH
Druck und Bindung: Books on Demand GmbH, Norderstedt Germany
ISBN: 978-3-656-71534-4

This book at GRIN:

http://www.grin.com/en/e-book/278066/behavioral-economics-lernzusammenfassung

GRIN - Your knowledge has value

Der GRIN Verlag publiziert seit 1998 wissenschaftliche Arbeiten von Studenten, Hochschullehrern und anderen Akademikern als eBook und gedrucktes Buch. Die Verlagswebsite www.grin.com ist die ideale Plattform zur Veröffentlichung von Hausarbeiten, Abschlussarbeiten, wissenschaftlichen Aufsätzen, Dissertationen und Fachbüchern.

Visit us on the internet:

http://www.grin.com/

http://www.facebook.com/grincom

http://www.twitter.com/grin_com

Inhalt

Zusammenfassung Behavorial Economics

1. Behavioral Decision Theory

- Standard economic model:
    - Descriptive theory: how people make decisions
    - Normative theory: how people should make decisions
- What makes a good theory:
    - 1. Congruence with reality: Explain or fit observations and make testable predictions that later prove to be correct. Models predictions should always be tested with new data that were not used to estimate the model originally
    - 2. Generality: Good theory applies to a wide selection of phenomena. Exp. Law of diminishing returns
    - 3. Tractability (Formbarkeit): Making testable predictions easily for different situations.
    - 4. Parsimony (Sparsamkeit): Occam´s razor: What can be done with fewer assumptions, is done vain with more.
    - 5. Precision: Ability to give exact numerical predictions about behavior (Exp. Nash equilibrium has a high precision)
    - 6. Psychological plausibility

1.1 Expected Utility Theory

$$\max_{x_i^t \in X_i} \sum_{s_t \in S_t} p(s_t) U(x_i^t | s_t)$$

The main components are

(1) $\max\limits_{x_i^t \in X_i}$ (2) $\sum_{t=0}^{\infty} \delta^t$ (3) $\sum_{s_t \in S_t} p(s_t)$ (4) $U(x_i^t | s_t)$

Three fundamental characteristics of decision-making:

- **Preferences** - rankings people have over a set of options or gambles that are based on attitudes and values related to the outcomes of these options (4)
- **Beliefs** – these relate to the probabilities with which people think various outcomes will occur, conditional on available information (3)
- **Rationality** – involves all four components of the model
  - Determine preferences based on attitudes and values (4)
  - Appropriately modify their beliefs in the light of new information (3)
  - Discount values of future outcomes (2)
  - Succeed in choosing optimal actions given preferences and beliefs (1)

Decision making under risk can be considered as a process of choosing between different **prospects** (gambles, lotteries). A prospect consists of a number of possible outcomes (x_i) along with their associated probabilities (p_i)

$$q = (x_1, p_1; ....; x_n, p_n)$$

Example: Prospects
Prospect A: 50% chance to win 100, 50% chance to win nothing --> q = (100, 0,5; 0, 0,5)
Prospect B: Certainty of winning 45 --> r = (45)

1.1.1 Axioms of Expected Utility Theory
- <u>Ordering</u> Axiom: Preferences for lotteries are complete and transitive
- <u>Continuity</u>: This assumption guaranties that preferences can be represented by some function that attaches a real value to every prospect
- <u>Independence</u> axiom: If two prospects are mixed with a third one, the preferences between the prospects don´t change.
  Example: q = (3000), r = (4000, 0.8) --> If q > r then q´ = (3000, 0,25), r = (4000, 0.2)
- <u>Monotonicity</u> (stochastic dominance)

$$\sum_{j=1}^{n} p_{qj} \geq \sum_{j=1}^{n} p_{rj} \quad for \; all \; i = 1, ... n \qquad \sum_{j=1}^{n} p_{qj} > \sum_{j=1}^{n} p_{rj} \quad for \; at \; least \; one \; i$$

Expected Utility Theory states that

- **Preferences of a rational individual can be described by a utility function $U: X \to \mathbb{R}$ such that**

$$r > s \Leftrightarrow \sum_{i=1}^{n} p(x_{ri}) u(x_{ri}) > \sum_{i=1}^{n} p(x_{si}) u(x_{si})$$

- Consumers **maximize their expected utility** when choosing between prospects. The expected utility of a prospect is:

$$U(x_1, p_1; \ldots; x_n; p_n) = p_1 u(x_1) + \cdots + p_n u(x_n) = \sum_{i} p_i u(x_i)$$

- Three further assumptions:
  - Invariance:
    - descriptive invariance: preferences should not depend on the description of the options
    - procedure invariance: preferences should not depend on the method of elicitation (Herausholen)
  - Asset integration
  - Risk aversion: a person is risk-averse if she prefers the certain prospect r = (x) to any risky prospect with expected value x. In EUT, risk aversion is caused by the concavity of the utility function

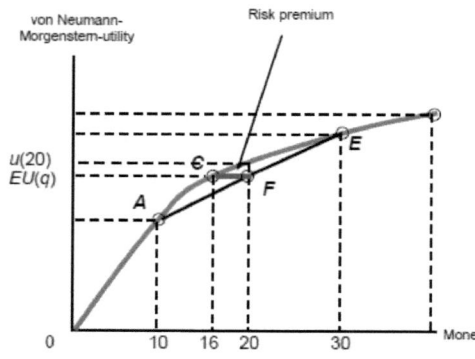

$q = (30, 0.5; \ 10, 0.5)$

expected value of q:
$E(q) = 20.$

Since the utility of the expected value $u(20)$ of the lottery is larger than the expected utility of the lottery $EU(q) = 0.5u(10) + 0.5u(30)$, the person is risk-averse.

The person would be willing to accept €4 less than the expected value to avoid the risk of the lottery. („risk premium").

1.2. Classical Anomalies

- Allais-Paradox: The Allais-Paradox violates the independence axiom and is an example of what is called consequence effect.

Decision problem 1 (DP1) Which lottery would you choose?	Decision problem 2 (DP2) Which lottery would you choose?
A: € 1000 with certainty	C: € 1000 with $p = 0.11$ 　　€　　0 with $p = 0.89$
B: € 1000 with $p = 0.89$ 　　€ 5000 with $p = 0.10$ 　　€　　0 with $p = 0.01$	D: € 5000 with $p = 0.10$ 　　€　　0 with $p = 0.90$

Individuals typically show the following pattern: $A > B$ and $C < D$.
This contradicts expected utility theory. Why?
We make the following normalization: $u(€5000) = 1$, $u(€0) = 0$, $u(€1000) = v$.
According to EUT:
$A > B \Rightarrow v > 0.89v + 0.10 \Rightarrow 0.11v > 0.10$
$C < D \Rightarrow 0.11v < 0.10$ **Contradiction!**

- Ellsberg-Paradox: 90 marbles in an urn, 30 red and 60 black and yellow, but in undefined relation. The majority chooses (1a) and (2b). This choice violates the independence axiom, because the number of yellow marbles is identical for a and b.

y ... number of yellow marbles

Game 1
Which alternative do you choose?
(1a) € 10 if a red marble is drawn
(1b) € 10, if a black marble is drawn

(1a) > (1b), if
$$\frac{30}{90} > \frac{60-y}{90} \quad y = \text{gelbe Kugeln}$$
$$\rightarrow y > 30$$

Game 2
Which alternative do you choose?
(2a) € 10 if red or yellow.
(2b) € 10 if black or yellow.

(2b) > (2a), if
$$\frac{30+y}{90} < \frac{60}{90}$$
$$\rightarrow y < 30$$

Interpretation: Individuals prefer risk over ambiguity (Doppeldeutigkeit).
　　Risk: Outcomes are uncertain, but probabilities are known
　　Ambiguity: Outcomes are uncertain, and probabilities are not known

1.3 Value formation

(1) $\max\limits_{x_i^t \in X_i}$ (2) $\sum_{t=0}^{\infty} \delta^t$ (3) $\sum_{s_t \in S_t} p(s_t)$ (4) $U(x_i^t | s_t)$

- <u>Attitude</u>:
  a psychological tendency that is expressed by evaluating. Objects of attitudes (entities) are mental representations
  - ○ <u>Preference</u>:
    In the standard economic model it is assumed that attitudes determine preferences
    - ▪ <u>Value = utility</u>:
      Quantitative evaluation that results from attitude. Usually what economists mean by the term utility
      - • <u>Choice</u>:
        Involves an action and a decision. Choice is a revealed preference

<u>**1.3.1 Menu effects**</u> -> violates generally the invariance assumption (relevant marketing practice)
- **Attraction effect (decoy effect)**:

  Consider the following subscription offers for "The Economist"

Economist.com offers		Price
Option 1	Web subscription	$59
Option 2	Print subscription	$125
Option 3	Print + web subscription	$125

  Choice frequencies of MBA students:
  Option 1 and 3 are available: 68% choose 1, 32% choose 3
  Option 1, 2, and 3 are available: 16% choose option 1, 0% option 2, 84% option 3

  ⇒ *The inclusion of an option that no-one would choose affects the preferences for the remaining options.*

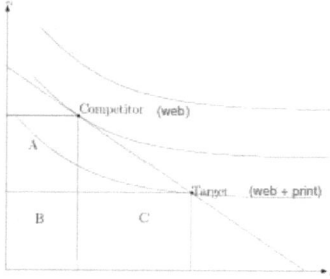

Introducing the decoy:
The decoy is dominated by the target (inferior in both dimensions), offers more x1 than the competitor. Introducing the decoy apparently shifts the indifference curves so that the preference between competitor and target becomes reversed.

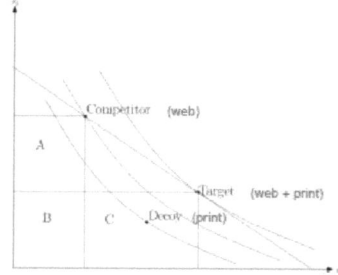

Example: Both your „target" product as well as the „competitor" product are within the individual's budget constraint. Individuals prefer the „competitor", thus it must lie on a higher indifference curve than the target.

6

- **Choice avoidance (paradox of choice):** Consumer compares the positive attributes of the alternative chosen to the union of the positive attributes of all alternatives not chosen. The opportunity costs that are considered increase in the options presented.

Study on consumer choice (Iyengar and Lepper, 2000).
Consumers in a supermarket were offered the opportunity to taste jams in two different treatments.

Treatment	Jams	Stoppers	Buyers
Simple (n=260)	6	40% (104)	30% (31)
Difficult (n=242)	24	60% (145)	3% (4)

1.3.2 Status Quo and endowment effect: nur für greifbare Dinge

The valuation of a good should be independent of owning the good or not. This implies that the maximum willingness to pay should be equal to the minimum willingness to ask. Empirical evidence, especially in experiments, consistently rejects this assumption. It indicates that gains (acquiring (=erwerben) a good) are evaluated differently from losses (giving up a good).

	Mean	Median
Selling Price	$5.78	$5.75
Buying Price	$2.21	$2.25

Results

Group	prefer mug over chocolate	prefer chocolate over mug
Group 1: No initial entitlement	56%	44%
Group 2: mug, (chocolate offered)	89%	11%
Group 3: chocolate (mug offered)	10%	90%

1.3.3 Preferences reversals

In a binary choice, attention is drawn to the gain probability. In valuation elicitation (WTA) attention is drawn to the gain amount

Choose between two lotteries:
> **$-bet:** A=(0.1; $140)
> **P-bet:** B=(0.8, $15)
1. Which lottery do you choose?
2. What is your minimum WTA to sell lottery A?
3. What is your minimum WTA to sell lottery B?

Typical result
- WTA for lottery A: $14, WTA for lottery B: $12, but choosing B over A.

- In binary choice, subjects prefer the P-bet, but assign a higher monetary valuation to the $ bet. This is inconsistent with rational choice, since the lottery with higher evaluation should be preferred.

Why?

Assume C=($13) (or any amount between 12 and 14), then the observed choice pattern would result in $B > A$, $A > C$, $C > B$, violating transitivity.

1.4 Probability judgment

1) $\max\limits_{x_i^t \in x_i}$ (2) $\sum_{t=0}^{\infty} \delta^t$ (3) $\sum_{s_t \in S_t} p(s_t)$ (4) $U(x_i^t | s_t)$

Concerning the point of beliefs, two assumptions are central to the standard economic model:

- Perfect rationality:
  Individuals don´t have all relevant information for making a decision, but also have the *cognitive abilities* to process it. The opposing concept is *bounded rationality*. You assume that people use simple heuristics (decision rules) when judging probabilities, instead of maximize their utility. The use of heuristics, however, often results in biases, meaning systematic errors.
- Bayesian probability estimation:
  Individuals are able to estimate probabilities correctly, given the relevant information. Bayes theorem:

$$P(A \mid B) = \frac{P(B \mid A) \cdot P(A)}{P(B)}$$

Hierbei ist

$P(A \mid B)$ die (bedingte) Wahrscheinlichkeit des Ereignisses A unter der Bedingung, dass B eingetreten ist,
$P(B \mid A)$ die (bedingte) Wahrscheinlichkeit des Ereignisses B unter der Bedingung, dass A eingetreten ist,
$P(A)$ die A-priori-Wahrscheinlichkeit des Ereignisses A und
$P(B)$ die A-priori-Wahrscheinlichkeit des Ereignisses B.

Bei endlich vielen Ereignissen lautet der Satz von Bayes:

Wenn A_i, $i = 1, \ldots, N$ eine Zerlegung der Ergebnismenge in disjunkte Ereignisse ist, gilt für die A-posteriori-Wahrscheinlichkeit $P(A_i \mid B)$

$$P(A_i \mid B) = \frac{P(B \mid A_i) \cdot P(A_i)}{P(B)} = \frac{P(B \mid A_i) \cdot P(A_i)}{\sum_{j=1}^{N} P(B \mid A_j) \cdot P(A_j)}$$

1.4.1 Representativeness heuristic

- Base rate neglect: Example with disease. 1 of 1000 got it and 5% false positive diagnostic tests --> bayesian theorem!!
- Conjunction effect: Example with Björn Borg. More detailed descriptions are judged as more likely or representative. (Teilmengen sind nicht größer als eine einzelne Menge)
- Small samples:
  People apply principles that apply to infinite populations also to small samples
  - Gambler fallacy: Heads or Tails. Sequence of HHH. Probability that H is coming next is also 50% as before. A couple of people would say that the probability is lower than 50%. --> Sequence doesn´t continue; *Reversion of a trend*.
    Explanation: relies on people´s assumption that signals are drawn from an urn of finite size and known distribution without replacement
  - Hot hand effect: Basketball fans think that a player´s chance of hitting a shot is greater following a hit than following a miss. --> Sequence continue; *continuation of a trend*
    Explanation: relies on people´s assumption that signals are drawn from an urn of finite size and unknown distribution without replacement

1.4.2 Availability and anchoring heuristic:

<u>Availability</u>: Probability judgment often have to be constructed and thus depend on how easy facts are available in memory.

<u>Anchoring and adjustment</u>: Example with wheel with random numbers and how much inhabitants does Cairo has. Random number and estimated inhabitants are highly correlated. Random number servers as a anchor, the adjustment is insufficient (mangelhaft).

1.4.3 Self-evaluation bias (egocentric bias)

<u>Overconfidence</u>: Individuals often overestimates their knowledge or abilities, i.e. they are too certain of their self. Three effects are distinguished:

- <u>Overestimation</u>:
  Refers to the overestimation of one´s actual ability, performance, level of control or chance of success.
- <u>Overplacement</u>:
  Refers to the better-than-average-effect.
- <u>Overprecision</u>:
  Refers to the excessive certainty in the accuracy of one´s beliefs

<u>Underconfidence</u>: Overconfidence is frequently found in easy tasks, underconfindence in difficult tasks.

<u>Explanation</u>:

- People have imperfect information about their own abilities and knowledge and even worse information about others
- People estimates of themselves are thus regressive (to the mean), and of others even more regressive

<u>Confirmatory (Bestätigung) Bias</u>: Refers to the tendency to interpret new, ambiguous information as being consistent with one´s prior beliefs. Other information won´t be recognized

<u>Self-attribution bias</u>: Refers to the tendency to discount information that is inconsistent with one´s prior beliefs.

1.5 Prospect Theory

1.5.1 General principles

- <u>Editing Phase</u>: To organize and reformulate the options so as to simplify subsequent evaluation and choice.
  - <u>Coding</u>: the outcome of a lottery are not considered in absolute terms but relative to a reference point, as gains and losses. By modifying the reference point, the decision frame and thus the expectations of the individual change.
  - <u>Combination</u>: Prospects with identical outcomes are simplified by combining probabilities.
    E.g. q = (200, 0,25; 200, 0,25) = (200, 0,5)
  - <u>Segregation</u>: Some prospects contain a riskless component that can be segregated from the risky component.
    E.g. s = (300, 0.80; 200, 0.20) is segregated to s´ = (200) and s´´ = (100, 0.80)
  - <u>Cancellation</u>: when different prospects share certain identical components, these components may be discarded or ignored.
    E.g. l_1 = (200, 0.2; 100, 0.5; -50, 0.3) & l_2 = (200, 0.2; 150, 0.5; -100, 0.3) is reduced to l_1 = (100, 0.5; -50, 0.3) & l_2 = (150, 0.5; -100, 0.3)
  - <u>Simplification</u>: Prospects are simplified by either rounding outcomes or probabilities. Sometimes simplification is done first.
  - <u>Detection</u> of <u>dominance</u>: Some prospects may dominate others, meaning that they have elements in common but other elements involve outcomes or probabilities that are always preferred.
- <u>Evaluation phase</u>: in this phase, the editing prospects are assigned a value, and subjects choose the prospect with the highest value V. The Value V of a prospect is expressed in terms of two scales:
  - v assigns a number to each outcome x of the prospect **v(x)** which reflects the <u>subjective value</u> of this outcome. This entails an explanation of **reference points, loss aversion and diminishing marginal sensitivity**
  - π associates a decision weight to each probability p: **π(p)** which reflects the impact of p on the overall value of the prospects. This entails an explanation of **decision weighting**.
- <u>Prospect Theory</u>: Mathematical exposition
  The typical utility function u(x) = x^b in the expected utility theory is replaced by the following value function:

$$v(x) = \begin{cases} (x - r)^\alpha & \text{if } x \geq r \text{ \small gain domain} \\ -\lambda(r - x)^\beta & \text{if } x < r \text{ \small loss domain} \end{cases}$$

with $\alpha, \beta > 0$.

There are *four parameters* in this model:

r…reference point
α…coefficient of diminishing marginal sensitivity for gains
β…coefficient of diminishing marginal sensitivity for losses
λ…coefficient of loss aversion <small>loss of 10$ hurts more than the joy of a gain of 10$</small>

  - α und β können gleich sein, ist aber überhaupt kein muss

The basic equation of Prospect theory describes the manner in which v and π are combined to determine the overall value of regular prospects. The value of regular prospects is:

$$V(x, p; y, q) = \pi(p)v(x) + \pi(q)v(y)$$

where $v(0) = 0$, $\pi(0) = 0$ and $\pi(1) = 1$.

Note that V is defined on prospects, whereas v is defined on outcomes. The two coincide for sure prospects, where

$$V(x, 1) = V(x) = v(x)$$

Example: A coin is tossed where the outcome of heads results in a gain of €20 while the outcome of tails results in a loss of €10. The utility of this regular prospect can be written as:

$$V(20, 0.5; -10, 0.5) = \pi(0.5)v(20) + \pi(0.5)v(-10)$$

The **value of a strictly positive (negative) prospect** with $p + q = 1$ and $x > y > 0$ (or $x < y < 0$) is:

$$V(x, p; y, q) = \overset{\text{riskless}}{v(y)} + \overset{\text{risky}}{\pi(p)[v(x) - v(y)]}$$

The value of a strictly positive or negative prospects equals the value of the riskless component plus the value difference between the outcomes, multiplied with the weight associated with the more extreme outcome.

Example:

$$V(400, 0.25; 100, 0.75) = v(100) + \pi(0.25)[v(400) - v(100)]$$

The value of strictly positive and negative prospects follow different rules. In the editing phase, such prospects are segregated into two components: the risky and the riskless component:

1.5.2 Loss Aversion

Illustration: Prospects of the form $s = (x, 0.5, -x, 0.50)$ are unattractive to most individuals.

Formally,
$$\frac{\partial v(x)}{\partial x} < \frac{\partial v(-x)}{\partial(-x)}$$

or
$$v(x) < -v(-x) \text{ where } x > 0$$

The **loss aversion parameter** λ can be expressed by:

$$\lambda = \frac{-v(-x)}{v(x)}$$

K & T have established a median value of 2.25

The utility function of the standard model has a concave shape (caused by the law of diminishing marginal utility) implying risk aversion at all levels of wealth.

Concave for gains and convex for losses

$$\frac{\partial^2 v(x)}{\partial x} < 0 \ for \ x > 0 \quad and \quad \frac{\partial^2 v(x)}{\partial x} > 0 \ for \ x < 0$$

gain domain   loss domain

This implies that diminishing marginal sensitivity generally causes risk-aversion in the domain of gains and risk-seeking in the domain of losses.

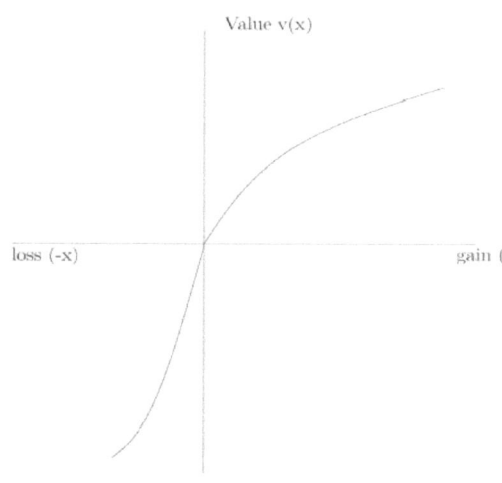

Value v(x)

loss (-x)

gain (x)

This value function is kinked at 0 (the reference point r), and is stepper in the loss domain than in the gain domain, referring to loss aversion.

$$v(x) = \begin{cases} x^{\alpha} & if \ x \geq 0 \\ -\lambda(-x)^{\beta} & if \ x < 0 \end{cases}$$

Exp.
Lottery: risky in gain domain
Insurance: risk avers in loss domain
Exp.
Choose between A = (4000, 0.8) & B = (3000)
Choose between C = (-4000, 0.8) & B = (-3000)
--> B > A (80%) but C > D (92%)

A hypothecial Prospect Theory value function

1.5.4 Decision weighting

For two reasons decision weights are different from objective probabilities:

- <u>Estimation</u> of <u>probabilities</u>:
  People are bad at estimating probabilities, they overestimate rare events and cannot perform Bayesian updating
- <u>Weighting</u> of <u>probabilities</u>:
  The decision weights measure the impact of events on the desirability of prospects (and not the perceived likelihood of these events)

The weighting function $\pi(p)$ is used instead of probabilities. $\pi(p)$ is a strictly monotonically increasing function with three characteristics:

- <u>Subadditivity</u>: (applies mainly to very small probabilities)
  Exp. : The lottery (6000, 0.001) is preferred to the lottery (3000, 0.002) by 72% of respondents. This choice pattern can´t be accounted for by diminishing marginal sensitivity (risk aversion for gains) alone. Concavity of the value function implies that:
  - **v(3000) > 0.5v(6000)** (in case of risk aversion), but the observed choice pattern is,
  - 0.001v(6000) > 0.002v(3000) --> **0.5v(6000) > v(3000)**
  Such a choice pattern can only be explained by a decision weighting function involving subadditivity
- <u>Subcertainty</u>:
  Subcertainty implies that individuals are less sensitve to variations in probability than expected utility theory (EUT) suggests. Graphically, this is illustrated in a decision weighting function $\pi(p)$ that is less step than the 45°line
  Exp. : The lottery (2400) is preferred to (2500, 0.33; 2400, 0.66) by 82%. But 83% preferred (2500, 0.33) to (2400, 0.34).
  - First case implies: $v(2400) > \pi(0.66)v(2400) + \pi(0.33)v(2500)$
  - Second case implies: $\pi(0.33)v(2500) > \pi(0.34)v(2400)$
  - Thus: $1 > \pi(0.66) + \pi(0.34)$
            --> Decision weights are smaller than 1, although there are 1
  - In general, subcertainty can be expressed as: **$\pi(p) + V(1-p) < 1$**
- <u>Subproportionality</u>:
  The prospect theory weighting function violates the independent axiom of EUT.
  Exp. :   (3000) > (4000, 0.8) | x 0.25
       (4000, 0.2) > (3000, 0.25)   situation changes when a common factor is introduced!
  The Subproportionality principle states that:

$$\frac{\pi(pq)}{\pi(p)} \leq \frac{\pi(pqr)}{\pi(pr)} \text{ for } 0 < p, q, r \leq 1$$

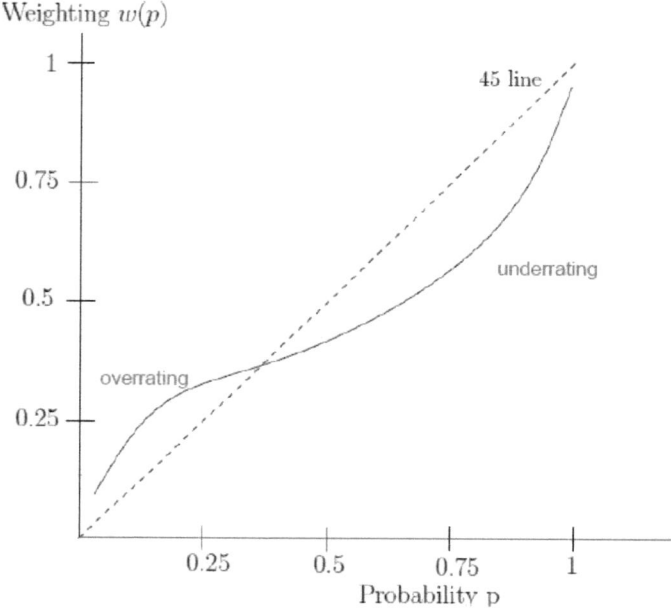

- <u>Cumulative</u> <u>Prospect</u> <u>Theory</u>:
  The general difference is that the principle of diminishing marginal sensitivity is applied to weighting functions as well as the value function. The decision weighting function is now denoted by w(p) and reflects an S-shape form:

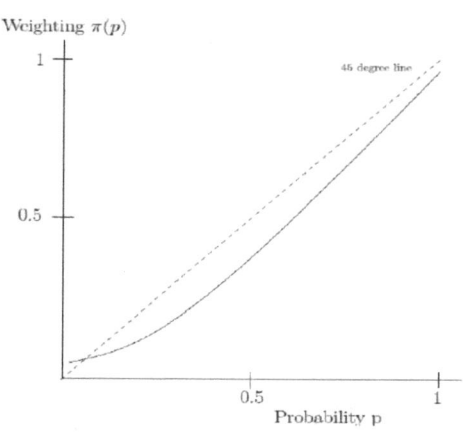

A hypothecial weighting function $\pi(p)$

Note that the weighting function has discontinuities at very low and very high probabilities.

- Events with very low probability are ignored.
- Events with very high probability are considered as certain.

The advantage of the function form of the decision weighting function w(p) are:
- o It requires only one parameter (parsimony)
- o can account for both, concave and convex regions
- o does not require symmetry around 0.5

With this model, some pattern can be explained, that seems to fit quite well with empirical observations:
- o Risk-aversion for gains of high probability
- o Risk-aversion for losses of low probability --> Exp. Insurance
- o Risk-seeking for losses of high probability
- o Risk-seeking for gains of low probability --> Exp. Lottery

Decision weighting function:

$$r = (100, p; 0, q)$$

Prospect Theory:

$$V(r) = \pi(p)v(x) = v(CE) \rightarrow \pi(p) = \frac{v(CE)}{v(x)} \qquad \pi(p) := \text{decision w. function}$$

Expected Utility Theory:

$$EU(r) = p * u(x) = u(CE) \rightarrow p = \frac{u(CE)}{u(x)} \qquad u(x) := \text{utility of non-zero outcome}$$

Probability	Domain of gains	Domain of losses
low	Risk seeking	Risk averse
moderate	Risk avers	Risk seeking
high	Risk avers	Risk seeking

1.6 Mental Accounting

Mental accounting means that individuals create different accounts for different entities. Mental accounts also relates to the *editing phase* of the Prospect Theory, because it determines weather assets are integrated or segregated. If they belong to the same account, they are integrated whereas if they belong to separate accounts, they are segregated.

<u>Hedonic editing</u>:
Segregate gains and integrate losses. According to Prospect Theory, segregating (integrating) gains (losses) yields higher utility/value than integrating (segregating) them.

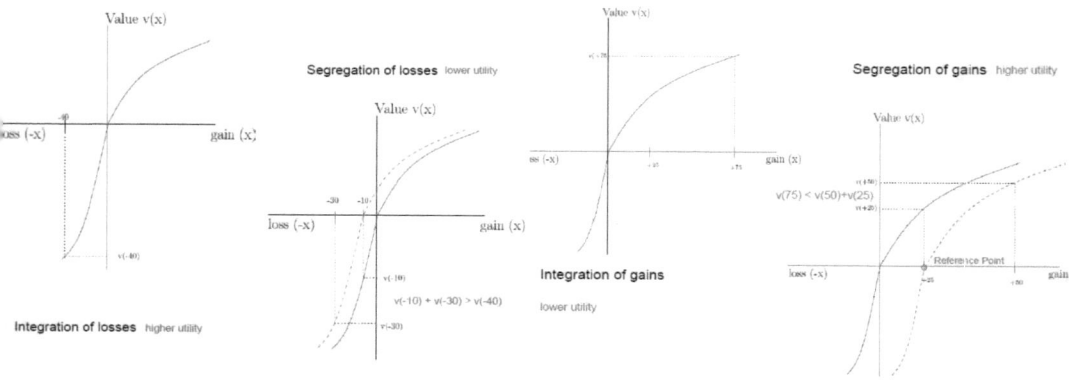

2. Intertemporal Choice and sustainable decisions

Until now we have considered outcomes that appear at the same time. Very often, decisions have consequences that occur at different points in time.

- Cases of immediate costs and deferred benefits (Sachen gleich erledigen):
  Savings behavior: favoring a later benefit (e.g. retirement consumption) over some immediate good (e.g. new car)
- Cases of immediate benefits and deferred costs (Sachen aufschieben):
  Procrastination: favoring immediate good (e.g. movie) over a later benefit (a clean flat)

2.1 The Discounted utility model (DUM)

$$\max_{x_i^t \in X_i} \sum_{t=0}^{\infty} \delta^t \sum_{s_t \in S_t} p(s_t) U(x_i^t | s_t)$$

δ....(time-consistent) **discount factor** with $0 < \delta < 1$ Was ist 1€ für uns morgen wert?!

$U(x_i^t | s_t)$...utility defined over the payoff x_i^t of individual i

The discounted utility model assumes that from the viewpoint of today, the utility of a Euro today is greater than the utility of a Euro tomorrow.

It proposes that the intertemporal utility function $U_t(c_t,....,c_T)$ captures the utility at time t of the consumption profile $(c_t, c_{t+1},....,c_T)$ starting in period t and continuing to period T.

$$U_t(c_t, ..., c_T) = \sum_{k=0}^{T-t} \delta^k u(c_{t+k})$$

If an individual discounts future utility at the rate of 10% per year, her discount factor is:

$$\delta = \frac{1}{1 + 0.1} = 0.91$$

where the **discount factor** δ can also be expressed in terms of the **discount rate** r

$$\delta^k = \left(\frac{1}{1+r}\right)^k$$

A simple time-discounting problem

Utility stream $u(c_t)$	$u(c_0)$	$u(c_1)$	$u(c_2)$	$\delta = 0.9$ $U_0(c_0, c_1, c_2)$	$\delta = 0.1$ $U_0(c_0, c_1, c_2)$
a	1			1	1
b		3		$0.9 \cdot 3 = 2.7$	$0.1 \cdot 3 = 0.3$
c			4	$0.9^2 \cdot 4 = 3.24$	$0.1^2 \cdot 4 = 0.04$
d	1	3	4	$1 + 0.9 \cdot 3 + 0.9^2 \cdot 4$ $= 6.16$	$1 + 0.1 \cdot 3 + 0.1^2 \cdot 4$ $= 1.304$

- If choosing between a, b and c, a decision maker with $\delta = 0.9$ chooses c, while a decision maker with $\delta = 0.1$ chooses a.
- A high δ (close to 1) indicates patience, a low δ (close to 0) indicates impatience.

2.1.1 Assumptions and features of the Discounted utility model:

- Integration of new alternatvies with existing plans
- Utility Independence :
  A persons utility is simply the sum of all the discounted future utilities
- Consumption independence:
  A person's welfare in any time period is independent of consumption in any other period.
- Stationary instantaneous utility:
  It implies that people's preferences do not change over time
- Stationary discouting:
  People use the same discount rate over their lifeplan. It has been shown, that children and old people are more impatience than middle aged people.

$$U_t(a_t) > U_t(b_{t+k}) \Leftrightarrow U_{t+j}(a_t) > U_{t+j}(b_{t+k})$$

An individual who discounts the future exponentially is time consistent.

$$U_t(a_t) > U_t(b_{t+k}) \Rightarrow u(a_t) > \delta^k u(b_{t+k})$$
Discounted utility

Now, what happens if we move in time? Would it be possible in $t-1$ to prefer the reward b at time $t+k$ over the reward a at time t?

This would imply that

$$U_{t-1}(b_{t+k}) > U_{t-1}(a_t) \Rightarrow \delta^{k+1} u(b_{t+k}) > \delta u(a_t)$$

$$\delta^k u(b_{t+k}) > u(a_t)$$

which is a contradiction to above.

- Constant discounting:
  At any period of time, the same per-period discount factor $\delta = \frac{1}{1+r}$ is applied to all future periods.
- Independence of discounting from consumption:
  All forms of consumption are discounted at the same rate.
- Diminishing marginal utility and positive time preference:
  - Diminishing marginal utility might cause people to delay consumption until later periods (e.g. leave some of the dinner for tomorrow)
  - Usually, time preference is assumed to be positive ($\delta > 0$, or $r > 0$, resp.) meaning that future utilities have less value

Time consistent preferences:

If an individual at time t prefers reward a at time t to reward b at time t+k, she should also prefer reward a at time t to reward b at time t+k at all points in time t+j (Präferenzen ändern sich über die Zeit nicht)

This implies, for instance, that your preference between an immediate and a delayed reward should never change when moving in time.

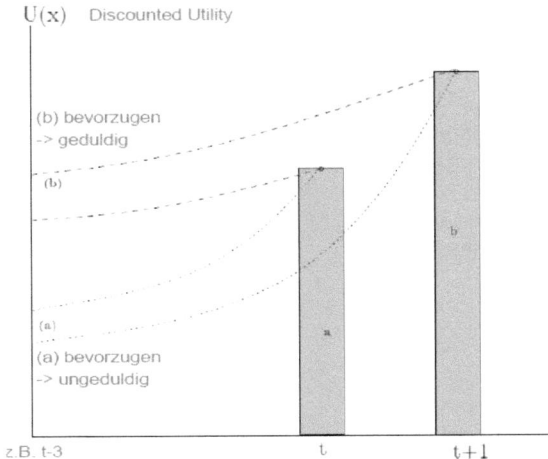

The strict preference between the two rewards can be like (a) or (b), but **time consistency** requires that the two lines will never cross.

(a) $U_t(a_t) > U_t(b_{t+1}) \Rightarrow$

$$u(a_t) > \delta u(b_{t+1})$$

(b) $U_t(a_t) < U_t(b_{t+1}) \Rightarrow$

$$u(a_t) < \delta u(b_{t+1})$$

Discount factor is higher in (b) than in (a).
In b the person is more patient

Labels in figure:
U(x) Discounted Utility
(b) bevorzugen -> geduldig
(b)
(a)
(a) bevorzugen -> ungeduldig
z.B. t-3
t
t+1
b
a

Example:

A subject matches the value of €500 in 10 years to €100 now. Beides gibt denselben Nutzen

The **discrete discounting model** would calculate the discount factor δ per year, respectively, the yearly discount rate r, to be: linear utility function -> weil hier nicht von Nutzen sondern von payoff ausgegangen wird (risk neutral)

weil jährlich gefragt

$$100 = 500 \cdot \delta^{10} \qquad \delta = \left(\frac{100}{500}\right)^{\frac{1}{10}} = 0.851 \qquad r = \frac{1}{\delta} - 1 = 0.175$$

The **continuous discounting model** would calculate discount factor δ to be the same. Yet, the yearly discount rate r would be:

$$\delta = 0.851 \qquad r = ln\left(\frac{1}{\delta}\right) = 0.161$$

Discount rates (corresponding to interest rates) are always lower when using the continuous discounting model.

2.1.3 Some anomalies in the Discounted Utility Model (DUM)

- Sign Effect:
  - Gains are discounted more than losses. I.e. discount factors that are elicited for the gain domain are lower than discount factors elicited for the loss domain.
  - To the extreme, many people prefer to experience a loss immediately than delay it, implying a discount factor of 1 for losses
- Magnitude Effect:
  - Patience is higher (δ larger) for larger amounts than for small amounts
  - Discounting is higher for small amounts than for large amounts (δ lower)
- Preference for improving sequences:
  - Subjects usually prefer increasing sequences
  - Yet this is not reconcilable with the DUM
- Violation of independence
- Preference for spread

2.2 Alternative intertemporal choice models

2.2.1 Time inconsistent preferences (bspw. Wecker auf 8e stellen, um 8e dann nicht aufstehen)

Two widely observed, empirical phenomena are not compatible with the Discounted Utility Model. Both can be summarized under the term "self-control problems":

- Temptation/Versuchung: Choosing between actions that have:
  - costs now and benefits later (e.g. investment in education)
  - costs later and benefits now (e.g. watching TV and eating junk food)

  Frequently the "costs" now involve opportunity cost of an unpleasant activity to gain a different benefit later

- Procrastination/Aufschieben: Exp. want to start learning at x-mas but starting later in reality

2.2.2 Hyperbolic discounting

- Present bias:
  People are more impatient in the short run (using a smaller discount factor for the immediate future) and become more patient over the long run (using a higher discount factor for the future that is further away)

The present value of the future outcome X in period t can be written as:

$$X = X_t \cdot \frac{1}{(1+r)^t} = \delta^t X_t$$

$\delta = \frac{1}{(1+r)} = 0.9091$ Discount factor per time period

$r = \frac{1}{\delta} - 1 = 0.1$ Discount rate per time period

$\delta^t = D(t) = 0.9091^t$ Discount function (on years t)

- (Quasi) Hyperbolic discounting:
  - discrete form:

$$D(t) = \begin{cases} 1 & if \ t = 0 \quad \text{present bias} \\ \beta \delta^t & if \ t > 0 \end{cases}$$

  - This model is often referred to as the (β, δ) −model.
  - It implies that utilities in periods 0,1,2,...t are discounted by $1, \beta\delta, \beta\delta^2, ..., \beta\delta^t$.
  - Generally, $\beta < 1$, implying that the discount factor between current period and next is lower than between future periods.
  - β measures the degree of present bias.
  - If $\beta > 1$ the model can also account for the reverse time inconsistency, such that later outcomes are preferred to sooner ones.

  - The discount factor between today (t = 0) and tomorrow (t = 1) is: $\beta\delta < 1$
  - The discount factor between tomorrow (t = 1)and the day after (t = 2) is:

$$\frac{\beta\delta^2}{\beta\delta} = \delta$$

$$\beta\delta < \delta$$

  - continuous form:

$$D(t) = (1 + \alpha t)^{-\frac{\beta}{\alpha}}$$

  - α determines how much the function departs from constant discounting.   beta = present bias
  - The limiting case of $\alpha \rightarrow 0$ is the exponential discount function (in its continuous form): $D(t) = e^{-\beta t}$
  - Implications of hyperbolic discounting: Examples

    Example 1 ("Temptation"): An individual discounts hyperbolically with $\beta = 0.6$ and $\delta = 0.9$. She is faced with a decision between receiving €100 in six years' time (the ss reward) and €200 in eight years' time (the ll reward).

    discounted utility beta delta
    $$U_0(ss) = 0.6(0.9)^6(100) = 31.9$$

    $$U_0(ll) = 0.6(0.9)^8(200) = 51.7$$

    At present time t=0, the individual chooses the larger, delayed reward of €200 in 8 years (ll). What about the decision when the six years have passed?

    $$U_6(ss) = 100 \quad \text{0.9^0 * 100 = 100 ; } \beta \text{ in t=0 --> 1}$$

    $$U_6(ll) = 0.6(0.9)^2(200) = 97.2$$

    After the six years, the individual's preference has reversed and she will choose the smaller, immediate reward.

Example 2 ("Procrastination"): An individual discounts hyperbolically with $\beta = 0.6$ and $\delta = 0.9$. She is faced with a decision between costs of €100 in six years' time (the ss cost) and €200 in eight years' time (the ll costs).

$$U_0(ss) = 0.6(0.9)^6(-100) = -31.9$$

$$U_0(ll) = 0.6(0.9)^8(-200) = -51.7$$

At present time t=0, the individual chooses the smaller, sooner costs in 6 six years. After six years have passed:

$$U_6(ss) = -100$$

$$U_6(ll) = 0.6(0.9)^2(200) = -97.2$$

After the six years, the individual's preference has reversed and she will choose to procrastinate, i.e. choose later costs.

The manner in which such inconsistency affects behavior depends on the degree of self-awareness (Ichbewusstsein) of subjects, in terms of how aware they are that their preferences will change over time:

- "Naive" type:
    o belief that their future preferences are equal to their present ones
    o this implies people don't learn from past experience of changing preferences over time
    o naive agents belief they are using a constant discount rate in the future, but will actually discount hyperbolically. In the previous example, we assumed a naive type. Their belief b about the present bias β is b = 1 > β (wenn sie denken das sie nicht inkonsistent sind)
- "Sophisticated" type:
    o Accurate (exakt) prediction of how their preferences will change over time
    o their belief b about the present bias is β = b < 1
    o They can pre-commit to a certain course of action to prevent them from a preference reversal later on

Example:

Assume $\delta = 0.9$ and $\beta = 0.5$. Let n be the number of servings consumed and p the *price per serving*. S is the small bag, L the large one. Because there is a bulk discount on the Large bag, $p_s = 1.5 \ p_l = 1$.

cost of purchasing chips:	$u_p = -np$	(small = -1.5; big = -2)
utility of consumption:	$u_c = 1 + 5n$	(small = 6; big = 11)
health outcome:	$u_h = 3 - 6n$	(small = -3, big = -9)

What are the possible decisions and their consequences?

Three decisions are possible:

S   purchasing a small bag, which limits the consumption to one serving in t=1, negative health outcome is experienced in t=2

L(1)   purchasing a large bag, and consume a single serving in t=1, the second serving is consumed in t=2, negative health outcomes are therefore experienced in t=2 and t=3

L(2)   purchasing a large bag and consume both servings in t=1, negative health outcome is experienced in t=2

st of purchasing chips:	$u_p = -np$	
ity of consumption:	$u_c = 1 + 5n$	
alth outcome:	$u_h = 3 - 6n$	

cost of purchasing chips:	$u_p = -np$	
utility of consumption:	$u_c = 1 + 5n$	
health outcome:	$u_h = 3 - 6n$	

tional consumers (exponential discounter), $\delta = 0.9$

t	S	L(1)	L(2)
0	up = -1.5	up = -2	up = -2
1	uc = 6	uc = 6	uc = 11
2	uh = -3	uh = $-3 + 6 = 3$	uh = -9
3		uh = -3	
J_o	$= -1.5 + 6\delta - 3\delta^2$ $= 1.47$	$= -2 + 6\delta + 3\delta^2 - 3\delta^3$ $= 3.64$	$= -2 + 11\delta - 9\delta^2$ $= 0.61$
U_1	no decision to make	$= 6 + 3\delta - 3\delta^2$ $= 6.27$	$= 11 - 9\delta$ $= 2.9$

ational consumer maximizes discounted utility in period t=0 by posing to buy a large pack and planning to consume one serving in and one in t=2. In t=1, sticking to the plan still yields the highest counted utility. The preference is time consistent.

cost of purchasing chips:	$u_p = -np$	
utility of consumption:	$u_c = 1 + 5n$	
health outcome:	$u_h = 3 - 6n$	

Sophisticated (hyperbolic) consumers, $\delta = 0.9, \beta = 0.5$

	S	L(1)	L(2)
	-1.5	-2	-2
	6	6	11
	-1.5	$-3 + 6 = 3$	-9
		-3	
	$= -1.5 + 6\beta\delta - 3\beta\delta^2$ $= -0.015$	$= -2 + 6\beta\delta + 3\beta\delta^2 - 3\beta\delta^3$ $= 0.82$	$= -2 + 11\beta\delta - 9\beta\delta^2$ $= -0.69$
		$= 6 + 3\beta\delta - 3\beta\delta^3$ $= 6.13$	$= 11 - 9\beta\delta$ $= 6.95$

A sophisticated consumer has complete knowledge of the change in utilities in the future and therefore realizes that she will change preferences at t=1. Since at t=0, L(2) is the worst of all options, the consumer wants to avoid this, and instead commit to S to prevent the switch to L(2) in the future.

present bias

Naïve (hyperbolic) consumers, $\delta = 0.9, \beta = 0.5$

t	S	L(1)	L(2)
0	-1.5	-2	-2
1	6	6	11
2	-3	$-3 + 6 = 3$	-9
3		-3	
U_o	$= -1.5 + 6\beta\delta - 3\beta\delta^2$ $= -0.015$	$= -2 + 6\beta\delta + 3\beta\delta^2 - 3\beta\delta^3$ $= 0.82$	$= -2 + 11\beta\delta - 9\beta\delta^2$ $= -0.69$
U_1		$= 6 + 3\beta\delta - 3\beta\delta^2$ $= 6.13$	$= 11 - 9\beta\delta$ $= 6.95$

A naive consumer maximizes discounted utility in period t=0 by choosing to buy a large pack and planning to consume one serving in t=1 and one in t=2. In t=1, changing the plan and consuming two servings immediately yields highest discounted utility.

- From the point of view t = 0, the naive consumer ends up worst
- the rational discounter ends up best
- the sophisticated ends up in between

3. Behavioral Game Theory

3.1 Nature of (Behavioral) Game Theory
Strategic interactions involve situations where the decision of one party affects another and vice versa.
Assumptions of standard and behavioral game theory:

Standard Game Theory (SGT)	Behavioral Game Theory (BGT)
1. People have correct mental representations of the relevant game	1. Representation: might be incomplete or not correct
2. People have unbounded rationality. actions match beliefs	2. Initial conditions: involve players belief about the game situation. Limits on strategic thinking or stochastic mistakes of individuals are assumed
3. Equilibria are reach instantly, learning is not modeled	3. Learning: players learn from others and their own strategies
4. People are motivated by pure self-interest	4. Social preferences: players care not only about their own payoff but also about others

3.2 Equilibrium concepts
1. Dominant strategy equilibrium:
A (weakly) dominant strategy is one that always gives at least as high a payoff as any other strategy, whatever the other player does. Each player will always choose the dominant strategy if there is one. The resulting equilibrium is one in dominant strategies.

*The strategy $s_i' \in S_i$ is **weakly dominant**, if for all strategies $s_i'' \neq s_i'$ with $s_i'' \in S_i$: $u_i(s_i', s_{-i}) \geq u_i(s_i'', s_{-i})$ for all $s_{-i} \in S_{-i}$.*

2. Iterated dominant strategy equilibrium:
Players will never play a strictly dominated strategy. One can eliminate all strictly dominated strategies for both players. If a single pair of strategies remains, this is an iterated dominant strategy equilibrium.

*A strategy $s_i' \in S_i$ is **strictly dominated**, if there exists another strategy $s_i'' \in S_i$ so that $u_i(s_i', s_{-i}) < u_i(s_i'', s_{-i})$ for all $s_{-i} \in S_{-i}$.*

3. Nash equilibrium:

Each player pursues the best strategy in response to the best strategy of the other player. Nash equilibria include equilibria obtained according to 1. and 2.but is a more general equilibrium concept.

> *The strategy profile s^* $\in$ S is a **Nash-equilibrium**, if for each player i the strategy s_i^* $\in$ S_i is a best response to the strategies s_{-i}^* $\in$ S_{-i} of all other players, that is, if $u_i(s_i^*, s_{-i}^*) \geq u_i(s_i, s_{-i}^*)$ for all s_i $\in$ S_i and for all i = 1, ..., n.*

> **Note:** *An equilibrium always consists of strategy tuple (one strategy for each player).*

4. Subgame perfect Nash equilibrium:

A subgame is the continuation game from a singleton node of a game tree to the end nodes which follow from that node. (A singleton node is one with no other node in its information set). Subgame perfection means that players play their equilibrium strategies if the subgame is reached. Players play their equilibrium strategies in each subgame. The solution concept to arrive at such an equilibrium is **backward induction**

> A **subgame** of a game in extensive form:

> a)   Starts at a decision node *k* in an information set with one element
> b)   Contains all decision and end nodes of the game tree that follow *k*
> c)   Does not separate any subsequent information sets

> A Nash-equilibrium is **subgame perfect**, if the strategies of the players are a Nash-equilibrium in each subgame (Selten 1965).

5. Mixed-Strategy Nash equilibrium:

Mixed strategies represent strategic uncertainty concerning the behavior of the other players. A pure strategy can be seen as a special case of a mixed strategy. All games have mixed strategies, but we look at games with discrete strategies.

> Let G = (N,S,u) be a normal form game with a finite strategy set S_i = $\{s_i^1, ..., s_i^m\}$. $s_i^1, ..., s_i^m$ are player i's **pure strategies**.

> A **mixed strategy** for player *i* is a probability distribution $p_i = (p_i^1, ..., p_i^m)$ over S_i, where $0 \leq p_i^k \leq 1$ and $p_i^1 + p_i^2 + ... + p_i^m = 1$.

A mixed strategy profile is thus a (mixed strategy) Nash equilibrium, if for each player, the expected payoff to every action to which a players strategy assigns positive probability is the same.

A mixed strategy profile $p* = (p_1*, ..., p_n*)$ is a **Nash-equilibrium** for a normal form game G, if for every player i the mixed strategy p_i* is a best response to the mixed strategies $p_{-i}*$ of the other players, i.e. if

$$u_i(p_i^*, p_{-i}^*) \geq u_i(p_i, p_{-i}^*) \text{ for all } p_i \text{ and all } i = 1, ..., n.$$

In an n-person normal form game G with a finite number of players n and finite strategy spaces S_i for all i, there exists at least one NE in pure or mixed strategies.

If players have doubts about the rationality of other players, there are some other strategies:

- Dominant strategy: does not require assumptions about the rationality of other players
- Maximin strategy: choose the strategy that maximizes the own minimum payoff

Example:

Consider the following symmetric 2-player game (Stahl and Wilson, 1995):

		Player 2		
		T	M	B
Player 1	T	25, 25	30, 60	100, 95
	M	60, 30	31,31	51, 30
	B	95, 100	30, 51	0, 0

- Three pure-strategy Nash-equilibria: (B,T), (M,M), (T,B)
- One is a *symmetric* pure strategy Nash-equilibrium: (M, M)
- Maximin strategy for each player: M

Observing strategy ‚M' in this game could indicate the attempt to coordinate on the unique symmetric pure strategy Nash-equilibrium or choosing Maximin strategy.

3.3 Bargaining

<u>Structured bargaining situation</u>: simple two-stage bargaining setting

In the first stage Player A makes a proposal how to split a pie of 5$. Player B can accept or reject. If player B reject, he can make a counter offer to player A in stage 2. Since there´s a cost of delay, the pie shrinks to 2$ in stage 2 (common discount factor δ = 0,4). If player A reject that offer both receive 0. Solution of the game using backward induction.

- In stage 2 player A would accept 0.01$ (0$), since he is better (equally) off than with rejection. Player B anticipates this and demand 1.99$ (2$) for himself
- In stage 1, player A anticipates that player B will accept nothing that makes him worse off than going to stage 2. Thus Player A will offer Player B 2$ and will demand 3$ for himself.
- The subgame perfect equilibrium is (offer 2$, accept)
- In general, Player A should offer the amount to which the pie is reduced in the second stage.

<u>Summary</u>:

- Players tend not to make equilibrium offers even when social preferences are not involved
- Players tend not to look ahead one or two stages to consider what will happen if an offer is rejected
- Players can learn to look ahead. I.e. using backward induction, if they are explicitly taught to do so.

3.4 Iterated dominance games

If games are not dominance solvable, i.e. there are no dominant strategies. The iterated elimination of dominant strategies might lead to an equilibrium.

Extensive form of the game

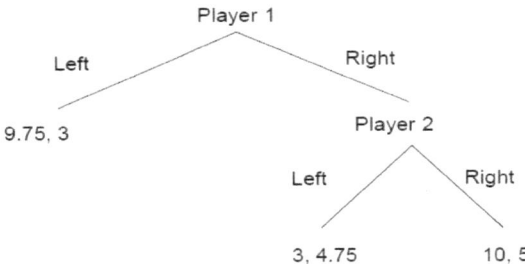

Only 66% of players 1 choose 'Right', since there is a risk in choosing 'Right' if player 2 does not obey dominance.

Only 83% of players 2 actually respond with 'Right' when Player 1 has chosen 'Right'.

⇨ *Players tend to believe that other players are less likely to obey dominance than they actually are.* Maximin-Strategy of P1: left

3.5 Models of bounded rationality (limited cognitive capacity)

Presently the most prominent models of bounded rationality are **level-k models** and the **Cognitive Hierarchy Theory**.

3.5.1 Level-k-Model

Subjects are classified into 5 main typed:

- Level-0: choose each possible strategy equally often (randomizers)
- Level-1: assume that others are Level-0 and the best respond to it
- Level-2: assume that others are Level-1 and the best respond to it
- Naive Nash: assuming others will play Nash
- Wordly Nash: assuming some others play Nash, but others are Level-1 or Level-2

Game 2 of Stahl and Wilson (1995)

		Player 2			
		T	M	B	3 NE: (T,T), (M,B), (B,M)
Player 1	T	75, 75	40, 70	45, 70	plausibel das (T,T) rauskommt
	M	70, 40	15,15	100, 60	auch Maximin (T, T)
	B	70, 45	60, 100	0, 0	

Predictions for different Levels:

Level-0:   uniform distribution of strategies $p_i = (^1/_3, ^1/_3, ^1/_3)$ mixed strategy

Level-1:   best response to level 0: $s_i = (M)$ $1/3 \cdot (70+15+100)$ am größten

Level-2:   best response to level 1: $s_i = (B)$ da Level-1 (M) nimmt

Naive Nash: $s_i = (T)$, since it is the unique symmetric NE strategy

Wordly Nash: $s_i = (M)$, assuming actual frequencies of Level 0 to 2 of others (without proof)

3.5.2 Cognitive Hierarchy Model

Assumes a **Poisson** frequency **distribution** of thinking **steps K** in the population. Those who use 0 steps correspond to Level-0 in the Level-K Model. Those who use K steps anticipate the decisions of all lower steps thinkers and best respond to the mixture of those decisions using normalized frequencies. It is parsimonious and easy to use because a Poisson distribution has only one parameter: mean and variance are identical (τ). In many games $\tau = 1.5$

- Minimizer Game with n-players (Bsp. aus Vorlesung mit 1€, 2€, 3€, diejenigen die das gewählt haben was am wenigsten gewählt wurde gewinnen)
- Nash -equilibrium prediction:
  - There are many (unplausible) asymmetric

Example: $N = \{1, 2, 3\}$
The mixed strategy Nash-equilibrium E is determined by the minimizer probabilities q_k satisfying $q_1 = 2q_2 = 3q_3$ and $\sum_k q_k = 1$.

$$q = (^6/_{11}, ^3/_{11}, ^2/_{11}).$$
lowest prob. of least often chosen at payout 3

- Poisson Cognitive Hierarchy prediction:
    - L0: choose every number with prob. 1/3 (randomizers)
    - L1: believe all others L0 and choices are uniformly distributed. Best response is therefore picking the highest number 3 to maximize expected utility
    - L2: believes all others are L0 and L1. The highest number 3 will therefore be most often chosen, 1 and 2 have equal prob. of turning out as the minimizer. Therefore choice of 2.
    - L3: believes all others are L0, L1 and L2 and opt for 1 as the minimizer
    - L4 and higher: choices depend on belief about frequencies of L0 to L3

The actual choice probabilities in the experiment can be compared with expectations that thinking steps are Poisson distributed with mean (variance) τ.
- The best fitting τ can be estimated by the distribution of choices.
- Observed choice frequencies can be tested against expectations that are derived from Camerer's postulation of $\tau = 1.5$.

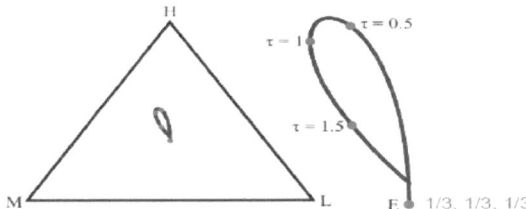

PCH-predicitons for different values of τ in the simplex

Expected and observed choice frequencies (in three large-scale experiments with varying payoff size, n=1360):

Payoff	Nash	PCH ($\tau = 1.5$)	Actual choice
100 Small	0.33	0.27	0.23
200 Medium	0.33	0.33	0.35
300 Large	0.33	0.41	0.42

Results reject Nash-play and confirm the PCH model with $1.20 \leq \tau \leq 1.52$.

- The minimizer game was designed so that social preferences (e.g. equality in payoffs) cannot play a role.

3.6 Signaling

Signaling might help overcome coordination problems, if there is a multiplicity of pure-strategy Nash-equilibria.

Stag-hunt game

		Player 2	
		Stag	Rabbit
Player 1	Stag	2, 2	0, 1
	Rabbit	1, 0	1, 1

(Stag,Stag) and (Rabbit,Rabbit) are both Nash-equilibria.
(Stag, Stag) is the payoff-dominant equilbrium, (Rabbit, Rabbit) the equilibrium in maximin strategies.

On which equilibrium will people coordinate?
- A large majority plays the inefficient equilibrium (Cooper et al., 1990)

How can the welfare maximizing equilibrium be reached?
- Signaling (i.e. indicating the intended strategy before playing the game) is **cheap talk**.
- Still, both sided signaling increases coordination on (S, S) to nearly 100%.

Most favored costumer clause (MFCC) --> Bestpreisgarantie:

- Each costumer gets the guarantee that the firm will not charge a lower price to other costumers for some period in the future.
- The strategy serves two purposes:
  o It creates good costumer relations
  o It creates a price commitment for the firm and signals to other firms that the price will be maintained. Thus the price under such a clause will be higher than without such a policy

Without MFCC		Firm 12	
		High Price	Low Price
Firm 1	High Price	50, 50	15, 70
	Low Price	70, 15	25, 25

The pricing strategies in an oligopoly market resembles a prisoner's dilemma.

A credible commitment (like the MFCC) changes the structure of the game to a coordination game with two pure-strategy equilibria.

With MFCC		Firm 12	
		High Price	Low Price
Firm 1	High Price	50, 50	10, 10
	Low Price	10, 10	25, 25

The MFCC serves as a signal to coordinate on (High Price, High Price).

- Two important characteristics of signaling:
  - o Affordability by the signaler´s type:
    To signal that someone is of a productive type, they must be able to afford the signal, i.e. make certain investment in education
  - o Non-affordability by other types:
    signaling high quality by giving a product warranty should not be affordable by producers with low quality.

3.7 Learning

Learning is ignored by standard game theory. (Nash)-Equilibrium is considered to be reached by deliberation and common knowledge or rationality.

<u>Summary</u>:

- Up to now, we have reviewed bounded rationality as limitations to cognitive capabilities.
- Models of Level-k-thinking steps or cognitive hierarchy capture the limits of rationality when it comes to applying the iterated dominance criterion or the Nash-equilibrium analysis
- Signaling and learning help to overcome coordination failure in games

4. Social preferences

The standard economic model involves pure self-interest, i.e. an individual´s care only about own (monetary) payoff. There are a lot of anomalies in daily life that cannot be explained if we take this assumption seriously. In fact, social preferences play a huge role for behavior in many strategic situations or n-players games.

4.1 Empirical evidence

- Ultimatum game:
  Player A: proposer, Player B. responder
  A gets an amount X (e.g. €10), which could be a surplus from trade or a gain to an exchange etc, and decides how to allocate X between herself and B. B can accept or reject.
  - If B accepts, the proposal is implemented: $x_A = (1 - s)X$, $x_B = sX$
  - If B rejects, both get nothing: $x_A = x_B = 0$

  x_i ... i's actual outcome, s ... B's share of X as proposed by A

  If both care only about their monetary payoff, what will they do? (anonymity, one-shot)

  - Assume 0.01€ is the lowest strictly positive amount
  - A self-interested B will strictly prefer to accept any strictly positive offer
  - Foreseeing this, A will never offer more than 0.01€. B will accept.
  - If A offers B 0.01€, B will accept.
  - If A offers B 0€, B might still accept, since she has nothing to gain by rejecting.

    o Nash-equilibrium: Set of strategies such that no player can profitably deviate from his strategy, given the strategies of the players.
    o Subgame-perfect Nash-equilibrium: eliminates Nash equilibria in which players threats are not credible (backward induction, Example above is a SPNE)
    o Summary of findings in the ultimatum game:
      - the majority of offers to the responder (60-80%) are between 40% and 50% of the total surplus
      - Almost no offers below 20%
      - Low offers are frequently rejected by responders. Offers <20% are rejected in about 50% of cases

- Dictator Game:
  The Dictator Game is variation of the ultimatum game, where player B has no right to reject. The proposal of player A is always implemented.
  Predictions with self-interested players:
    o The (selfish) proposer will demand the whole amount for himself: $x_A = c$, $x_B = 0$
    o In the dictator game, player A has no strategic reason to deviate the amount. The allocation of player A reflects pure preferences.

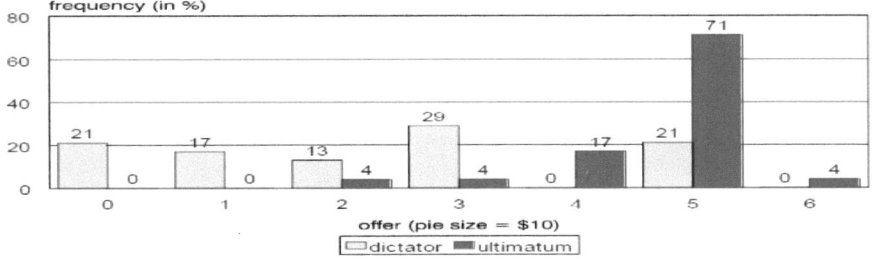

frequency (in %)

offer (pie size = $10)

dictator ■ultimatum

Dictators offer on average 20%, much lower than proposers in the ultimatum game

- Trust game (Investment game):
  Player A sends an amount to player B. The amount sent is multiplied, there is an efficiency gain by sending. Player B can send back any amount up to the received one to player A, and keeps the rest to himself.

  Think of the following example:
  A investor (trustor), **B** manager (trustee, who cannot be monitored)
  1. A has initial amount X, which he can choose to invest or keep.
  2. A invests $T \geq 0$ of this, which corresponds to sending to B. Player A keeps $(X - T)$.
  3. Investment T yields return $(1 + r)$, with $r > 0$, so B receives $(1 + r)T$
  4. B keeps Y of these earnings, and thus repays $(1 + r)T - Y$ to player A.
  5. Final payoffs:

  $$x_B = Y$$

  $$x_A = X - T + (1 + r)T - Y = X - Y + rT$$

  T is a measure of trust (or generosity?)
  $(1 + r)T - Y$ is a measure of trustworthiness (or generosity?)

  Summary of findings in the trust game:

  - A vast majority of trustors sends money: reflects unconditional kindness or trust
  - Trustees send back money: reflects unconditional kindness or trustworthiness
  - On average: Player A (investor) gets back the amount that is sent
  - Trust games allowed to investigate reciprocity

- Gift-exchange game:
  Models the interaction between employer and employee.

  Stage 1: Employer (player A) offers wage w.

  Stage 2: If a worker (player B) accepts the offer, she has a fixed cost for working of c and chooses effort level e, which is associated with costs $m(e)$, $m'(e) > 0$. If the worker does not accept, both earn nothing.

  Payoffs:

  $$u_W = w - c - m(e_w) \qquad \text{Worker}$$

  $$\pi_E = (v - w)e_w \qquad \text{Employee}$$

  where v may be interpreted as the revenue of the employer; one unit of effort produces v units of output which is sold for a price of one.

  Predictions with self-interested players:

  Workers will choose minimum effort e_{min}. The employer anticipates this and offers a wage that covers the workers fixed cost of working.
  Minimum wage

  o Results:
    - Reciprocity works: the higher the wage the higher the effort level
    - Subgame perfect Nash equilibrium: e* = e^min = 0.1, w* = reservation wage = 30
    - --> inefficient
- Prisoners Dilemma game

		Suspect B	
		Confess	Deny
Suspect A	Confess	-5, -5	0, -10
	Deny	-10, 0	-1, -1

  Two suspects are interrogated simultaneously about a joint crime. The payoffs represent years in prison, with -5 representing a 5 year prison sentence.

  Nash-equilibrium (in dominant strategies): (Confess, Confess) which is a defecting strategy.
  The 'cooperative' strategies (Deny, Deny) would result in a lower prison sentence for both.

  o Findings in the prisoners dilemma game:
    - In one shot games, players cooperate about half of the time
    - Pre-play communication that should not affect outcomes at all, has a significant effect in terms of increasing cooperation

- Public Good game:
  - Public goods have the characteristic of **non-exclusivity** (cannot easily provided to one person and not to others) and **non-depletion** (consumption of the goods does not reduce the amount of the good available to others), e.g. street lights.
  - For semi-public goods, there is a rivalry in consumption, i.e. the consumption of one individual causes a negative externality on another individual (i.e. library, stadiums, roads, hospital)
  - Non-exclusivity creates an incentive to free-ride, since everyone would be better off individually to consume the good but not pay for it. (i.e. groupwork)
  - A public good game reflects the same incentive structure as a (multi-person) prisoners dilemma game, but allows different levels of cooperation
  - Each of n players has an endowment of z and invests c_i of this resource in a public good that is shared to everyone.

Payoff of player i:

$$\pi_i = (z - c_i) + \frac{m}{n} \sum_{j=1}^{n} c_j \ \ with \ 0 < \frac{m}{n} < 1 < m$$

$\frac{m}{n} = a$ ...marginal per capita return

Optimal contribution for a self-interested player:

$$\frac{\partial \pi_i}{\partial c_i} = -1 + \frac{m}{n} < 0 \ since \ \frac{m}{n} < 1$$

$$c_i^* = 0$$

Socially optimal contribution:

$$\frac{\partial \sum_{i=1}^{n} \pi_i}{\partial c_i} = -1 + n\frac{m}{n} > 0 \ since \ m > 1$$

-1 + m > 0 --> m > 1

upper bound of endowment --> z

$$c_i^{**} = z$$

A public good game reflects the same incentive structure as a (multi-person) prisoner's dilemma game, but allows for different levels of cooperation.

Findings in the Public Good Game (Fehr and Gächter, 2000)

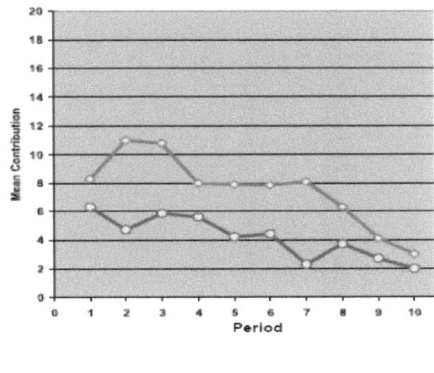

- repeated game over 10 rounds with constant groups (partners) or varying groups (strangers)

- about 40%-50% cooperation in first round

- decreasing cooperation

- endgame effect

- partners cooperate more than strangers (strategic cooperation to trigger further cooperation of others)

— Partners   —○— Strangers

35

4.2 Factors affecting social preferences

- <u>Repeating and learning</u>:
  Throughout repetitions of PG and bargaining games, outcomes tend to come closer to standard game theoretic predictions.
- <u>Stakes</u> (10$, 20$, 100$, 1000$,...)
  In bargaining games, stakes do not seem to play a large role.

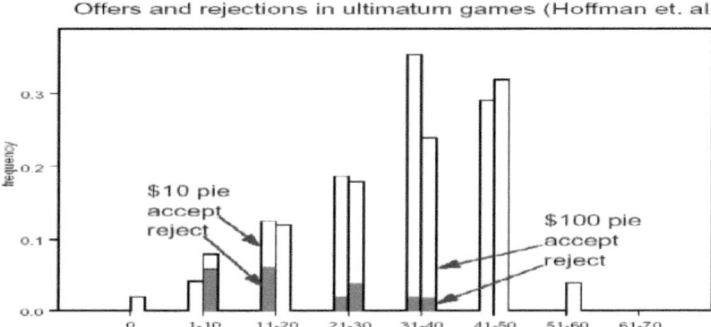

- <u>Anonymity</u>:
  - o The knowledge that their identity may be known either to the investigator or to other subjects may cause subjects to want to appear nice or please others.
  - o In dictator games, double blind procedures reduce sharing, while in situations of strategic interactions there is hardly any effect.
- <u>Communication</u>:
  - o Pre-play communication (cheap talk) has an augmenting effect on cooperation and dictator giving
- <u>Entitlement (Anspruch)</u>:
  - o Entitlement, e.g. by winning the role as proposer in the ultimatum game through the contest decreases offers. The perceived legitimacy of entitlement is not shared by responders since rejection rates are considerably high.

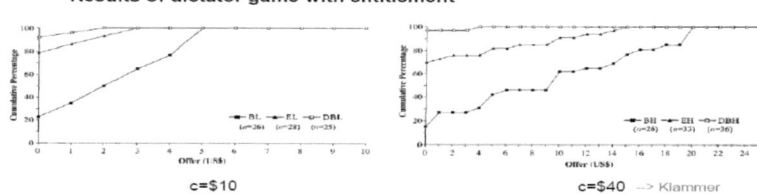

Results of dictator game with entitlement

c=$10 c=$40 ---> Klammer

BL.. Baseline, EL..Earned wealth, DBL...Double blind earned wealth

Results:

In the baseline, a zero offer is made in 21% (17%) of cases.

In the earned wealth treatments, this fraction increases to 80% (70%), and in the earned wealth double blind procedure, the fraction increases to 92% (98%).

Conclusion: If wealth is earned, sharing behavior comes close to standard game theoretic predictions.

- Competition:

  Ultimatum game embedded in a market context (Roth et al, *AER* 1991)

  In a group of n players, there are n-1>1 proposers (sellers) and one responder (buyer). The proposers compete to divide a cake c with the responder.

  Stage 1: Proposers simultaneously offer a split of *c* to the responder.

  Stage 2: Responder accepts or rejects best offer (rejection implies $y_i = 0 \ \forall i$). In case of a tie, one offer is chosen at random.

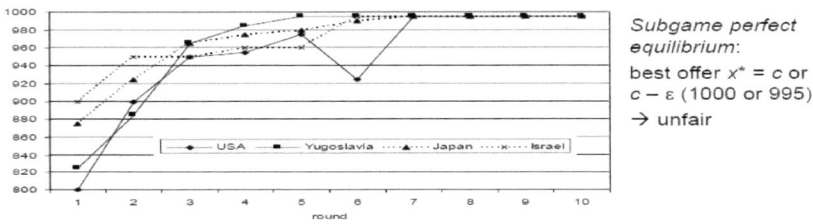

  Subgame perfect equilibrium:

  best offer $x^* = c$ or $c - \varepsilon$ (1000 or 995)

  → unfair

  ⇒Competition affects the judgment of fairness.

- Available Information:
  - The information available is the basis of social comparisons
  - Information about past behavior of players can be used to build up reputation and increase cooperation
  - In bargaining games, for instance, respondents may have different information about the size of the pie
    - Perfect information: the pie size is known for certain
    - incomplete information: the pie size and their probability distributors are known
    - no information
  - In cases of incomplete and no information, minimum acceptance thresholds (Grenze) of responders tend to be lower and proposers tend to exploit (ausnutzen) this
- Intentions:
  - Humans place great importance on the intentions behind a person´s action as well as on consequences
  - A persons perception of being treated unfairly seems to cause more outrage than the perception of unequal payoffs
- Opportunity (and cost) of punishment:
  - Desire for punish harmful behavior is stronger than the desire to reward friendly behavior.
  - Punishment might be defined as retaliation (Vergeltung) or as negative reciprocity
- Summary:
  - Anti-social punishment is rare in the western world. In eastern/southern cities this kind of punishment is more frequently observed
  - Factors that are related to anti-social punishment are a lack of trust and weak social norms of cooperation
  - Weaker social norms are prevalent in countries where exchange outside the extended family is rare. In developing countries, infrequent exchange outside the (large) family results in little experience and trust.

4.3 Modeling social preferences

The failure of game theory to predict many empirical outcomes may have two reasons:

- People do not engage in strategic thinking in practice, which means game theory is an in appropriate analytical technique
- Preferences are not modeled correctly, i.e. social preferences have to be taken into account

4.4 Inequality aversion models

4.4.1 The inequality aversion model of Fehr & Schmidt, FS-Model

- Individuals (2 player) consider their own income and the inequality between on income and others income.
- Individuals distinguish between advantageous inequality (own payoff is higher than others payoff) and disadvantageous inequality (others payoff is higher than own payoff)
- Utility function is linear:

$$U_i = x_i - \alpha_i \cdot max\{x_j - x_i, 0\} - \beta_i \cdot max\{x_i - x_j, 0\}$$

where x_i is the monetary payoff of individual i and $i \neq j$.

α_i ...'*envy*' parameter

β_i ...'*guilt*' parameter.

- Individuals suffer more from disadvantageous inequality: $\beta_i \leq \alpha_i$
- Individuals suffer from advantageous inequality: $0 \leq \beta_i < 1$
- The population of players is heterogeneous, i.e. different players have different values of α and β. Thus, α and β have distributions in the population rather than single values.

Utility function under FS-preferences

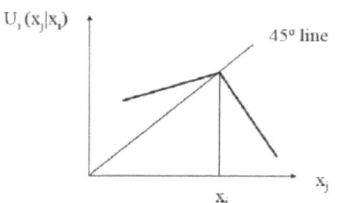

Individual *i* has the highest utility if the payoff of individual *j* is equal to his own. The utility of individual *i* decreases with the payoff difference. The decrease in utility is stronger if the payoff difference is disadvantageous for individual *i*.

- <u>FS-Model with n players</u>:
  Inequality aversion is normed by the number of other players. Each player compares himself to the others, but is not concerned by inequality across others

$$U_i(x_i) = x_i - \alpha_i \frac{1}{n-1} \sum_{j \neq i} max\{x_j - x_i, 0\} - \beta_i \frac{1}{n-1} \sum_{j \neq i} max\{x_i - x_j, 0\}$$

- <u>Properties and predictions of the FS-model</u>:
    - o the model is simple in terms of the parameters involved and the linearity of the function
    - o Predictions for public good games:
        - Free-riding if $\beta_i < 1 - m$, where m is the marginal return from the public good (and m/n is the marginal per capita return)
        - The number of free-riders k that causes everyone to free ride: $k > m(n-1)/2$
        - For given parameters m and c (cost of punishment), how much envy α_i and guilt β_i is necessary for an equilibrium to emerge where there are some positive contributors and punishment
- <u>Inequality averse proposer (with FS preferences)</u>:
  Proposer A, prefers high payoff for himself and equality between him and responder B. The pie size to allocate is c
    - o Proposed share s = 0.5:
      If the offer is accepted, this results in maximum equality but less than maximum payoff
    - o Proposed share s > 0.5:
      If the offer is accepted, this results in less payoff than under s = 0.5 and less equality. Both egoistic and inequality averse responders will accept s = 0.5. Proposer will never choose an offer of s > 0.5
    - o Proposed share s < 0.5:
      If offer is accepted, this results in a higher payoff than with s = 0.5 but less equality. Utility for proposer A for s < 0.5, given the responder accepts:

$$U_A = x_A - \alpha_A \max\{x_B - x_A, 0\} - \beta_A \max\{x_A - x_B, 0\}$$

$$= (1 - s)c - \beta_A[(1 - s)c - sc]$$

$$= c(s(2\beta_A - 1) - \beta_A + 1)$$

--> Ableitung nach s: c2betaA - c > 0 --> 2betaA > 1
--> betaA > 1/2 --> s at max = 0.5

The utility of A increases in s if $\beta_A > 0.5$

➤ If acceptance of B does not play a role (dictator game), proposer A would choose an offer of s=0 if $\beta_A < 0.5$, s=0.5 if $\beta_A > 0.5$ and would be indifferent between any offer $s \in [0, 0.5]$ if $\beta_A = 0.5$

Proposer A must consider, whether B will accept.

Assume that the following inequality averse preferences are *common knowledge*:

$$\alpha_A = \alpha_B = 2, \beta_A = \beta_B = 0.4$$

- Because $\beta_A < 0.5$, the proposer would prefer to keep the total pie c for himself despite his inequality aversion

Responder
- But Proposer B will reject, if

$$s < \frac{\alpha_B}{1 + 2\alpha_B} = \frac{2}{5} = 0.4$$

Proposer A anticipates this and offers s=0.4

Responder B will accept the offer.

Thats the equilibrium of the game

Equity - Reciprocity - Competition (ERC)

- Let's consider an n player lab game (i = 1,2,...,n) with anonymity and incomplete information
- The model assumes a motivation function (similar to a utility function):
  Player i maximizes the expected value of $v_i = v_i(y_i, \sigma_i)$, where $y_i \geq 0$ is i's absolute payoff

$$\sigma_i = \sigma_i(y_i, c, n) = \begin{cases} \dfrac{y_i}{c} & if\ c > 0 \qquad \text{c = cake} \\ \dfrac{1}{n} & if\ c = 0 \end{cases}$$

is i's share of the cake (relative payoff)

$c = \sum_{j=1}^{n} y_j$ is the total pecuniary payout (cake)

- Assumptions about the motivation function:
  - A0: v_i is continuous and twice differentiable
  - A1: Narrow self-interest:
    v_i increases in the absolute payoff y_i and if $v_i(y_i', \sigma_i) = v_i(y_i'', \sigma_i)$ and $y_i' < y_i''$ then i chooses (y_i'', σ_i)
  - A2: Comparative Effect:
    v_i decreases as the relative payoff σ_i moves away from the social reference share 1/n

$$\frac{\partial^2 v_i}{\partial \sigma_i} < 0, \frac{\partial v_i}{\partial \sigma_i} = 0 \text{ for } \sigma_i(y_i, c, n) = \frac{1}{n}$$

Note that $y_i \equiv c\sigma_i(y_i, c, n)$

Define:

Maximallohn
$$r_i(c) := \underset{\sigma_i}{argmax}\ v_i(c\sigma_i, \sigma_i)\ \ if\ c > 0$$

$$s_i(c):\ \ v_i(cs_i, s_i) = v_i(0, 1/n)\ \ if\ c > 0, s_i \leq 1/n$$
share of the cake when the share is fair. Same utility if c get 0 when everyone gets 0

$r_i \in [1/n, 1]$ corresponds to the division that i fixes in the dictator game.

$s_i \in [0,1/n]$ corresponds to i's rejection threshold in the ultimatum game.

  - A3: Heterogeneity:
    Let f and g be density functions; c > 0:
    - $f(r_i \mid c) > 0$ on [1/n, 1] and
    - $g(s_i \mid c) > 0$ on [0, 1/n]
    ERC provides a way to capture the incomplete information about how players trade off payoffs. All statements describe ERC-equilibria = perfect Bayesian equilibria with motivation functions

- Example:

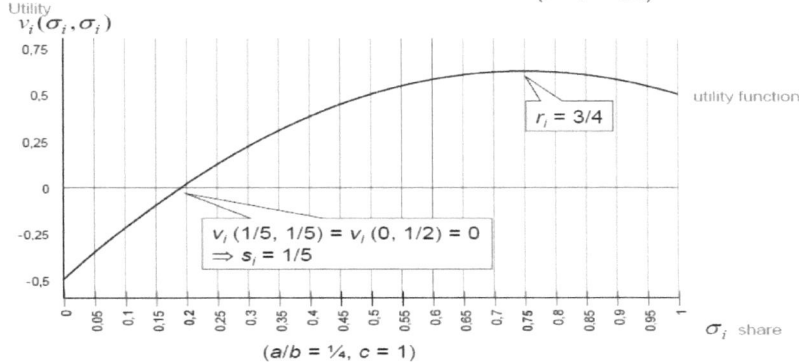

Example: Two-player game

$$v_i(c\sigma_i, \sigma_i) = a_i c\sigma_i - \frac{b_i}{2}\left(\sigma_i - \frac{1}{2}\right)^2 \; ; \; a_i \geq 0, b_i > 0$$

- strict narrow self interest:
  $b \to 0$
  ($r = 1$ and $s \to 0$)

- strict relativism: $a = 0$
  ($r = s = 1/2$)

Utility
$v_i(\sigma_i, \sigma_i)$

$r_i = 3/4$

utility function

$v_i(1/5, 1/5) = v_i(0, 1/2) = 0$
$\Rightarrow s_i = 1/5$

σ_i share

($a/b = \frac{1}{4}$, $c = 1$)

- Differences between the FS-Model and the ERC-Model:
  - ERC is concerned with relative shares, FS is concerned with absolute differences
  - ERC makes only a comparison between an individual's payoff with the average payoff of all other player. It does not compare each players payoff with the maximum and minimum of the other players, like FS.
  - ERC proposes a symmetrical attitude towards inequality (guilt and envy are equal in force), whereas FS proposes that envy is stronger than guilt
- Illustration: Three-person game with an allocation $(x, x - \varepsilon, x + \varepsilon)$
  - ERC: The preferences of the first player should be independent of ε since the sum of payoffs is constant and therefore the relative share of the first play is not affected
  - FS: as ε increases, envy of the third player's payoff and guilt regarding the second player's payoff both increases causing the first player's utility to fall.

The FS-Model seems to perform slightly better than the ERC-Model in a variety of games. Still, also the FS-Model us not universally valid.